Kids On Earth

A Children's Documentary Series Exploring Global Culture & The Natural World

Philippines

Sensei Paul David

COPYRIGHT PAGE

Kids On Earth - A Children's Documentary Series Exploring Global Cultures & The Natural World: Philippines

by Sensei Paul David,

Copyright © 2024.

All rights reserved.

978-1-77848-748-4 KoE_Phillipines_Ingram_HardbackBook

978-1-77848-747-7 KoE_Phillipines_Ingram_PaperbackBook

978-1-77848-746-0 KoE_Phillipines_Ingram_eBook

978-1-77848-745-3 KoE_Phillipines_Amazon_PaperbackBook

978-1-77848-744-6 KoE_Phillipines_Amazon_eBook

This book is not authorized for free distribution copying.

www.senseipublishing.com

@senseipublishing
#senseipublishing

Get Our FREE Books Now!

kidsonearth.life

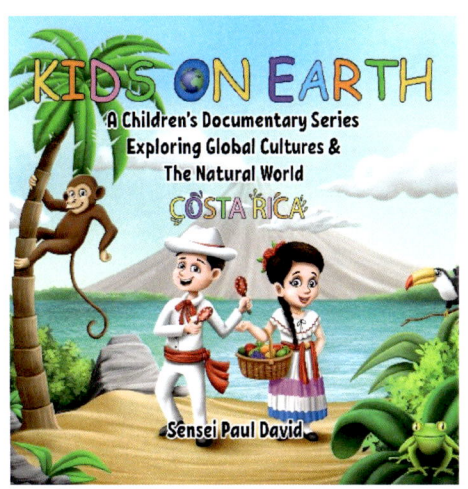

kidsonearth.world

Click Below or Search Amazon for Another Book In Each Series

Join Our Publishing Journey!

If you would like to receive FUTURE FREE BOOKS and get to know us better, please click www.senseipublishing.com and join our newsletter by entering your email address in the pop-up box.

Follow Our Blog: senseipauldavid.ca

Follow/Like/Subscribe: Facebook, Instagram, YouTube: @senseipublishing

Scan the QR Code with your phone or tablet to follow us on social media:

Like / Subscribe / Follow

Welcome to The Philippines!

My name is Perlah and this is my brother Arturo.

The Philippines is a small island country that can be found in the Pacific Ocean. The Philippines makes up an archipelago of islands that contain over 7,000 islands!

The capital of the Philippines is Manilla which is located on Luzon Island.

Arturo and I would love to take you on a trip through our beautiful country. It is a very special place, and we cannot wait to share it with you.

Are you excited? Let's Go!

FUN FACTS

The Philippines is named after Philip the Second who was king of Spain during the 16th Century, or from the years 1500-1600.

Remember how we said that the Philippines makes up part of an Archipelago? An Archipelago is another word for a big group of islands.

The largest island is called Luzon, and the second largest island is Mindanao.

Over 57% of the population in the Philippines can be found on the island of Luzon.

If you look at the fun facts, there are some interesting words.
Can you with the help of a grown-up find out the meaning of the following words?
1. **Province**
2. **Municipalities**
3. **Barangays**

FUN FACTS

The islands that make up the Philippines can be broken into eight separate regions. Inside these regions are 38 provinces, 74 cities, and 697 municipalities. There are also nearly 21 000 Barangays

The flag of the Philippines is an interesting design. The national flag has 4 colors!

There are horizontal stripes of blue and red, a white triangle, and then a golden sun with 3 stars.

The flag has some special meanings and became the flag of the Philippines in 1898.

The white triangle is a symbol of liberty, the sun and stars represent the 3 main areas of the Philippines, the sun has 8 rays which stand for the 8 provinces that started the revolution against Spain, and the blue stripe reminds us of the sacrifice for freedom, and the red symbolizes courage.

Have a look at your flag.
Are there any symbols on it? Symbols can be shapes,
animals, plants, or other art.

FUN FACTS

The blue on the flag has changed a few times over the years. In 1985 the president of the Philippines thought it should be light blue instead of dark, then it was changed back to dark blue by the next president before it was changed to another blue in 1997.

The people of the Philippines are called Filipinos. Filipinos are mainly made up of people who are descended from Malay.

The Malay people once lived on the Malay Peninsula, as well as in Borneo and Sumatra. The language spoken by the Malays varies and belongs to a special group called the Austronesian family of languages.

Filipino society has over 100 different cultural and language groups. Some of these are:
- The Tagalog who can be found in Luzon
- The Cebuano who makes up the language and culture group of the Visayan Islands
- The Ilocano can be found in the Northern parts of Luzon, and
- The Hilgaynon of the Bisayan Islands

With a grown-up's help, are you able to print a
Map of the Philippines, and using different colors
Mark where the different groups mentioned can be found.

FUN FACTS

So many different cultures and languages make up the Philippines. It helps make the Philippines a unique place to visit.

The Philippines has one primary religion that many follow, Roman Catholic, but there are other smaller religions that some of the population follow. This includes some indigenous religions, as well as religions bought from other countries such as Islam.

What do you know about the origins of your religion?
You might need to ask a grown-up to help you do some research and find the answers.

FUN FACTS

In 1902 the Philippine Independent Church also known as the Aglipayans, was founded in protest against the Spanish control of the Roman Catholic Church.

The Philippines has a great education system. The education system has been influenced by its Colonial History.

In 1898 English was introduced as the primary language that the students would be taught, and it was through the influence of America, that we have continued to learn English.

Until recently, the Philippines had the best education system in Southeast Asia.

When you finish school what would you like to learn as a job?

FUN FACTS

The Philippines has the shortest terms of education. We go to Primary school for 6 years, then high school for 4 years, before going to University for another 4 years.

The land that makes up the Philippines is diverse. The group of islands has the Philippine Sea to the east, the Celebes Sea to the South, the Sulu Sea to the Southwest, and the South China Sea to the West and North.

When you look at the islands from the sky, you will see that it looks like a triangle. It is about 1 150 miles or 1 850 kilometers from north to south, and at the widest point is 700 miles or 1 130 kilometers.

Looking at your country, does it make a special shape when you look at it from the sky?

FUN FACTS

The archipelago has 22 550 miles or 36 290 kilometers of coastline altogether! That is a lot of coastlines. But we also have coastal plains, mountains, rivers, and lakes. There are so many interesting places to see when you visit our Islands.

Because of where in the world our islands are, our climate is tropical, and we experience monsoons. From May to October, we have rain and lots of wind from the Southwest, and from November to February, we have dry winds from the Northeast.

> Perlah, that is an interesting word, Monsoon. Can you please help our readers with what a Monsoon is?

> Of course! A monsoon is where we get lots and lots of rain, and the winds can bring down trees. Sometimes, because it rains so much, we get flooded.

Time to do some research!
With a grown-up's help, using the internet, can you find videos of a Monsoon?

FUN FACTS

The strongest Monsoon in the Philippines is called Amihan. The Amihan is the Northeast Monsoon. The Southwest Monsoon is called Habagat.

When you visit the Philippines, remember to bring lots of pesos to buy the treasures you find.

The peso is the official currency of the Philippines. Unlike the Spanish American Peso which is symbolized by $ the Filipino Peso symbol is ₱

The central bank of the Philippines is called Bangko Sentral ng Pilipinas.

You may have seen the Peso in other countries, such as Spain. Originally we used to trade and barter different goods for other items, but it started to get too hard, so thanks to the Spanish, we introduced the Peso to help us buy and sell different items.

Our pesos can be broken down into the following:
- 20 Piso and is Orange
- 50 Piso and is Red
- 100 Piso and is Violet
- 200 Piso and is Green
- 500 Piso and is Yellow and
- 1 000 Piso which is Light Blue

Does your country release special items to remember some of the country's important dates?

FUN FACTS

To help celebrate special occasions, the Bank releases commemorative banknotes. We have had the 2000 Piso to help celebrate the Centennial of the Declaration of Philippine Independence in 1998, the 100 000 Piso for the Centennial of Declaration of Philippine Independence in 1998, and in 2021 we had a Quincentennial Commemoration note of 5 000 Piso

On one of our islands, the island called Palawan, there is an underground river that runs 24 kilometers and 14 miles. It is millions of years old and has some beautiful caves to explore.

The river is now a part of the UNESCO World Heritage Sites.

Looking at your country, do you have any sites that are protected by UNESCO?

FUN FACTS

UNESCO stands for United Nations Educational, Scientific and Cultural Organization. It helps protect the natural wonders around the world. UNESCO was founded in London, the United Kingdom in 1945

Some of our islands have some fascinating facts about them. You have just read about the island called Palawan, now we are going to share an interesting fact about another island, called Camiguin.

Camiguin is a really small island, only 14 miles long or 24 kilometers and 8.5 miles or 13 kilometers wide.

Camiguin is known around the world for having the most volcanoes on an island, around the entire world!

The Volcanoes have been dormant since 1950, so it is safe to come and explore this magical little island.

Perlah, what does dormant mean?

When the specialist called Volcanologists call a volcano dormant, it means that the volcanoes are sleeping. They could erupt one day, but for now they are quiet.

With a grown-up's help. You can look up on the internet How to Make a Volcano. It is a fun experiment to try!

FUN FACTS

Some interesting facts about volcanoes are:
1. that Lava can reach temperatures of up to 1200 degrees or 2192 Fahrenheit.
2. The Ash from the volcano can cause lightning.
3. Without the activity from volcanoes, our islands and continents would be a lot smaller. An example of this is Hawaii. Hawaii is made up of dried volcano flow.

Do you like playing basketball? The Philippines is the home of the first Asian Basketball League. It is also one of the oldest leagues in the world!

When you visit the Philippines you will find not only proper basketball courts but also make-shift ones everywhere.

Basketball, although founded in Springfield, America, by James Naismith in 1891. It was brought across to the Philippines and at first was only for women. This eventually changed, and it is now the National Sport of the Philippines.

What is your country's national sport?
Do you know its history?

FUN FACTS

Basketball was originally a winter sport. James Naismith was asked to invent a game that could be played during the wintertime. The restless college students needed a new sport that helped them burn off the energy and excitement that came with their summer sports.

Have you ever heard of a Jeepney?? No?

A Jeepney is a mode of transport that can only be found in the Philippines!

Jeepneys were created by resourceful Filipinos after America left behind thousands of jeeps at the end of World War 2. Jeepneys are part jeep and part bus and can transport up to 20 people.

Looking at the transportation in your country, what do you know about its history?
Do you know how many of each transportation modes there are?

FUN FACTS

There are currently 158,000 traditional Jeepneys on the road in the Philippines, with another 5,300 modern jeepneys that have air conditioning on the road.

Perlah and I have already mentioned the national flag, and sport. But we would like to share some more facts about our national icons.

- The National Anthem is called Lupang Hinirang. The national anthem was composed by Julian Felipe and was first played publicly in 1898
- The National Flower is called the Sampaguita. Another name for this flower is Arabian Jasmine.
- The National Tree is the Narra or the rosewood.
- The National Bird is the Philippine Eagle.
- The National Gem is the Philippine Pearl.

Do you know what your country's national symbols are?

FUN FACTS

The world's largest pearl was discovered by a Filipino diver in a giant Tridacna (mollusk) under the Palawan Sea in 1934.

The Philippines is one of the world's most diverse countries with its biodiversity.

Because of how big the biodiversity is in the Philippines; it is classified as a megadiverse country. There are nearly 5,000 endemic species of plants, marine ecosystems, and 700 threatened animal species all living in the Philippines.

Can you find the other megadiverse countries?
What makes them unique enough to be called a megadiverse?

FUN FACTS

There are 17 megadiverse countries around the world. Due to their own unique and individual ecosystems, each country has earned the name of Megadiverse.

Another interesting fact about the Philippines is that Filipinos make up a large percentage of nurses around the world.

Between 1903 and 1940 the United States opened up a study abroad program that was aimed at training internationals or those who came from different countries as nurses.

Does your country have training programs like they have in the Philippines?

FUN FACTS

During the training of Filipino nurses, the education was changed to suit the patients that the nurses would encounter. They were taught more about tropical diseases and industrial and living conditions within the islands.

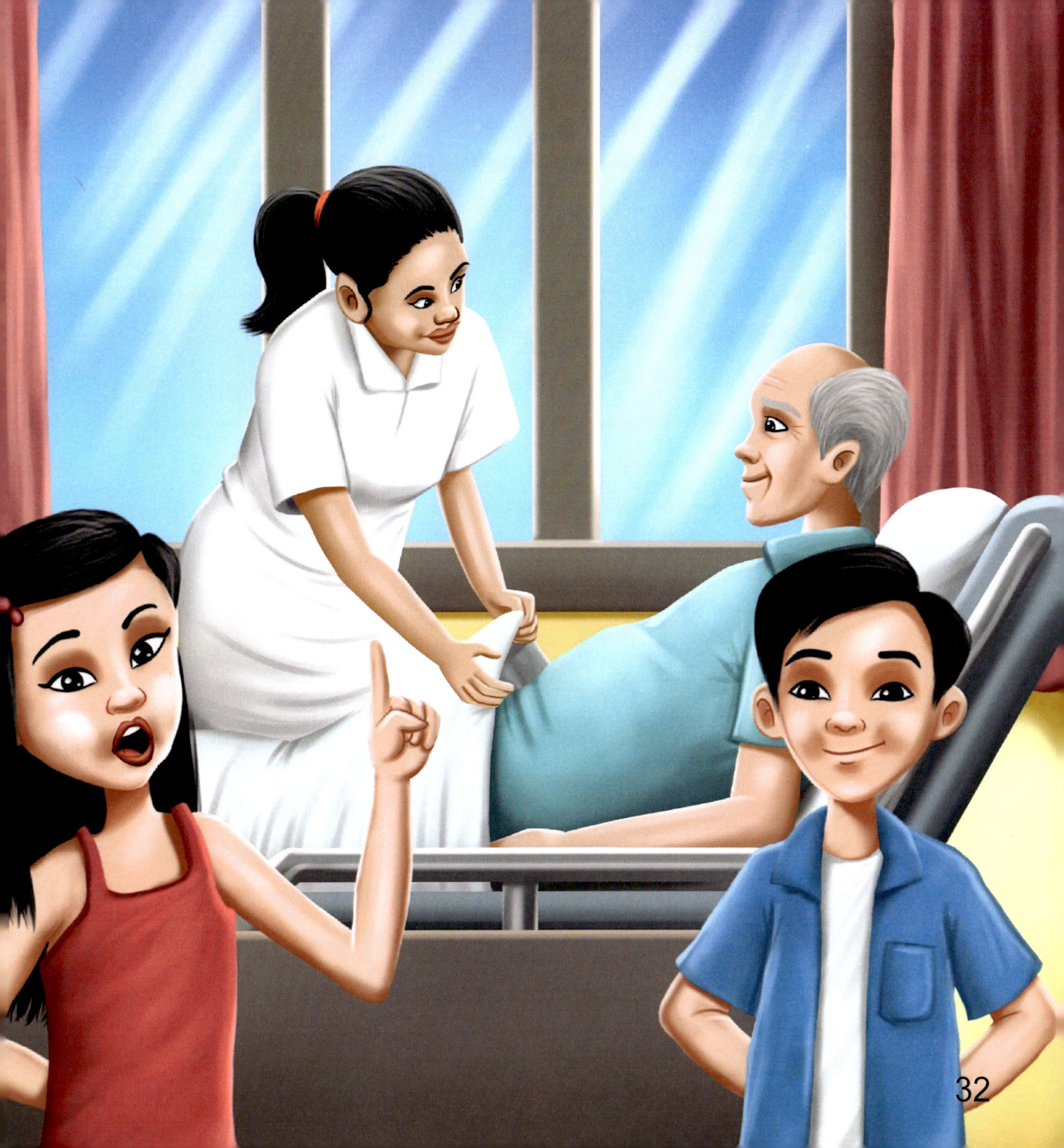

Do you like Coconuts? They are so delicious and refreshing. The Philippines is the world's second-biggest producer and exporter of coconuts, or around 19.5 million that get shared around the world!

Another name for the Coconut Tree is the tree of life. This is because it helps bring in jobs and money for most of the Philippines.

Have you ever eaten a coconut the way it is found in nature?
Your local produce or grocery shop might have one you can try.

FUN FACTS

Coconuts are a versatile fruit. Once you open it up you can use the 2 halves as bowls, and if small, as cups. Another great fact about coconuts is if you burn the husk it wards off insects.

Mmm, coconuts! Did you know that in the Philippines we have 4 meals a day? We have breakfast, morning tea, lunch, and 'merienda' or an afternoon meal or snack.

One thing that you will see in every meal, is rice!

Our national food is Adobo. It is a mix of different herbs and spices made into a yummy sauce, that meat marinades in, then it is cooked in a clay pot.

What is your national dish?

Would you like to try something different? With a grown-up's help, find a recipe for Adobo and cook it for dinner.

FUN FACTS

Different areas of the Philippines have their variation on Adobo.
Some places add soy sauce, some add ginger, and others use coconut milk.

Time to sing a song. An important part of Filipino culture is Karaoke. Everyone gets in and has a go.

It doesn't matter if you can sing or not, we all love to get together and sing along to some great songs. You will find that in some of our homes, we have a dedicated hut where we hold our karaoke nights.

Do you like to sing? What is your favorite song?

Wouldn't it be awesome to have a karaoke party?
Talk with a grown-up and see if you can have a party where everyone is singing.

FUN FACTS

The first karaoke machine was built by a Japanese inventor, Daisuke Inoue. Filipino inventor, Roberto del Rosario, patented the machine and is also responsible for the Karaoke Sing-Along System back in 1975.

We all love a good holiday. In the Philippines the longest holiday celebrated is Christmas. For, us Christmas begins in September, and during this time we have several different activities that we can all partake of.

Some of our other holidays are:
- Maundy Thursday in April to celebrate the events before Jesus was sacrificed.
- Araw ng Kagitingan in April also known as The Day of Valor. This is to remember those who have fought in wars and the War Veterans.
- Eid'l Fitr varies and is for our Muslim community. It helps them celebrate Ramadan.
- National Heroes Day in August
- Bonifacio Day in November to remember the birth of Andres Bonifacio.
- Rizal Day in December which is to remember Jose Rizal

In your country, do you have a special day to celebrate something special in your country?

FUN FACTS

Maundy Thursday is also known as Easter, and The Day of Valor is known as ANZAC Day in Australia.

There is so much to see on all the Islands that make up our home.

We have unusually named hills, rice terraces, volcanoes, rivers, lakes, reefs, waterfalls, monuments, forts, ruins, shrines, bridges, palaces, and churches.

Some of these places are called:
- Chocolate Hills
- Binondo Church
- Rice Terraces in Cordilleras

Do you have anywhere special like the rice terraces, where you live?

FUN FACTS

The rice terraces in Cordilleras were declared a National Treasure, and are also protected by the Republic Act, which provides protection and conservation of the National Cultural Heritage.

Like most countries, the Philippines has its national dress. The Filipino National Dress is called the baro't saya.

It is a mix of Filipino and Spanish clothing styles. The words Baro at Saya come from the Tagalog language and mean blouse and skirt, which are the main components of the outfit.

What is your national dress like?

Finding an image on the internet, with a grown-ups' help, can you put together the Filipino national Dress?

FUN FACTS

The Filipino president, Ferdinand Marcos, issued the decree that made the Baro't Saya would become the national dress, and that during the 5th and 11th of June would belong to the Baro't Saya.

Now that we have sung some songs, would you like to learn our National Dance?

The National Dance is called the Tinikling and is performed with bamboo poles. It is one of the oldest dances in the country. You can find this dance now, all over the world.

Where you live, do you have a special dance?

Maybe with a grown-up's help, you can find some videos on the Tinikling Dance and can try this at home.

FUN FACTS

The dance received its name from the Tikling Bird. The Tikling Bird belongs to a species of birds referred to as Rail Birds.

In the Philippines, our homes are built to withstand the weather.

Our homes are called Bahay Kubo or Nipa Hits. These houses sit on stilts, and the design can be dated back to the pre-Hispanic era.

Bahay Kubo means country house and refers to where homes were originally built. Most homes have 3 separate sections, the middle of the home is the living area, then we have a space above that is called the attic, and then below the house under the stilts is known as the Silong.

What type of homes do you have where you live?

FUN FACTS

The pre-Hispanic era refers to the time before the first Spanish settlement in 1521.

There are so many different animals that call the Philippines home.

There are over 200 known species of mammals alone, that can be found all over the Philippines and the islands around it.

Some of the animals we have are:
- Water Buffalo
- Pangolins
- Lemurs
- Chevrotains or Mouse Deer
- Mongooses
- Civet Cats and
- Monkeys

Can you think of any funny names of animals that don't look like what they sound like?

FUN FACTS

The mouse deer is not a deer! This little critter is known as the Pilandok in Filipino and is a small nocturnal ruminant.
A ruminant is a hooved animal with four stomachs.

Have you ever heard of vascular plants? A vascular plant is a special plant that has a series of tubes that connect all the different parts of the plant. This is to help move different nutrients and water from one part of the plant to another.

In the Philippines, we have more than 9,000 vascular plants that make up the flora found. That one-third of Al the plant life is found within the Philippines and her islands.

What is plant life like where you come from?

FUN FACTS

Within the Philippines and its vast landscapes is a plant called the Rafflesia Consueloae. The Rafflesia flower is the world's largest flower measuring 1.5 meters or 5 feet in diameter.

Rafflesia flower

Living on an Island means we are surrounded by lots of water. The Philippines sits between the South China Sea and the Pacific Ocean.

We also have a lot of water that can be found on the land, and these are called lakes. Unlike the ocean which is Sat Water, most of our lakes are freshwater lakes.

The smallest lake in the Philippines is the Jamboree Lake which is 1.5 hectares, and the biggest lake is Laguna da Bay which is 900 square kilometers or 350 square miles. That's a lot of water!

Do you have any lakes where you live?
What is the smallest lake and which is the largest?

FUN FACTS

The oldest lake in the Philippines is called Lake Lanao. Not only is it the oldest, but it is also the second-largest lake in the Philippines.

Looking back on history, Arturo found some interesting facts that he wanted to share with you.

Before the Philippines gained independence in 1946, we were the first US Colony in 1898.

The Philippines was also the first Southeast Asian Country to gain its independence.

And before we became known as Filipinos we were once called Pacific Islanders.

No one likes to talk about war. Has your country ever fought in a war that changed its History?

FUN FACTS

In 1898 Spain gave the US the Philippines, and then 48 years later when Japan tried to take over, the US stood beside the Filipinos in the war. After they won, the US granted the Filipinos independence.

Perlah would like to share with you her favorite thing about the Philippines.

Filipinos have a worldwide reputation for being polite. When you talk with a Filipino, you will find that they use Ma'am and Sir.

Between siblings, we use 'ate' and 'kuya' to show respect to the eldest siblings and we use 'po' and 'opo' to show respect towards older people.

What is your country like for being polite?
Do you try and use your manners when talking with others?

FUN FACTS

Filipinos are a very relaxed set of people. We sometimes can show up an hour or even two hours after the time we have been asked to.

You have made it to the end! We do hope that you enjoyed your journey and learned a lot of new and exciting facts about our beautiful home in the Philippines!

We just wish we had more time to tell you more!

Visit us at www.senseipublishing.com and sign up for our newsletter to learn more about our exciting books and to experience our FREE Guided Meditations for Kids & Adults.

As always…
It's a great day to be alive!
.

What have you learned?

Take this fun quiz to see how much you have remembered.

1. What is the National Dress called?
   a. Barot Saya
   b. Grass Skirts And Coconut Shells
   c. Shorts and T-Shirt
   d. Long Robes

2. When did the Philippines gain independence
   a. 1915
   b. 1898
   c. 1946
   d. 1846

3. How many mammals were mentioned?
   a. 2
   b. 4
   c. 3
   d. 7

4. Which oceans do the Philippines lay between?
   a. Pacific and Atlantic?
   b. South China and the Pacific
   c. Indian and Atlantic Ocean

d. Indian and South China
5. What fruit is the most sold in the Philippines?
   a. Mangoes
   b. Bananas
   c. Apples
   d. Coconuts

6. What color is the 200 Peso?
   a. Blue
   b. Yellow
   c. Green
   d. Red

7. What can you share with your friends that you have learned from this book?

Quiz Answers: 1A 2C 3D 4B 5D 6C

Thank you for reading this book!

If you found this book helpful, I would be grateful if you would **post an honest review on Amazon** so this book can reach other supportive readers like you!

All you need to do is digitally flip to the back and leave your review. Or visit amazon.com/author/senseipauldavid click the correct book cover and click on the blue link next to the yellow stars that say, "customer reviews."

As always...

It's a great day to be alive!

Share Our FREE eBooks Now!

kidsonearth.life

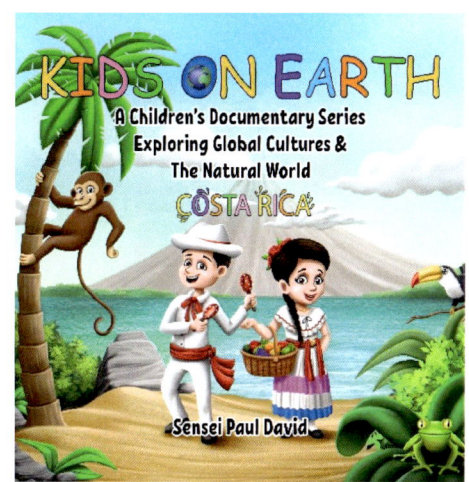

kidsonearth.world

Click Below or Search Amazon for Another Book In Each Series Or Visit:

www.amazon.com/author/senseipauldavid

www.senseipublishing.com

@senseipublishing
#senseipublishing

Check out our **recommendations** for other books for adults & kids plus other great resources by visiting
www.senseipublishing.com/resources/

Join Our Publishing Journey!

If you would like to receive FREE BOOKS and special offers, please visit www.senseipublishing.com and join our newsletter by entering your email address in the pop-up box

Follow Our Engaging Blog NOW!
senseipauldavid.ca

Get Our FREE Books Today!

Click & Share the Links Below

FREE Kids Books

lifeofbailey.senseipublishing.com

kidsonearth.senseipublishing.com

FREE Self-Development Book

senseiselfdevelopment.senseipublishing.com

FREE BONUS!!!

Experience Over 25 FREE Engaging Guided Meditations!

Prized Skills & Practices for Adults & Kids. Help Restore Deep Sleep, Lower Stress, Improve Posture, Navigate Uncertainty & More.

Download the Free Insight Timer App and click the link below:
http://insig.ht/sensei_paul

About Sensei Publishing

Sensei Publishing commits itself to helping people of all ages transform into better versions of themselves by providing high-quality and research-based self-development books with an emphasis on mental health and guided meditations. Sensei Publishing offers well-written e-books, audiobooks, paperbacks, and online courses that simplify complicated but practical topics in line with its mission to inspire people toward a positive transformation.

It's a great day to be alive!

About the Author

I create simple & transformative eBooks & Guided Meditations for Adults & Children proven to help navigate uncertainty, solve niche problems & bring families closer together.

I'm a former finance project manager, private pilot, jiu-jitsu instructor, musician & former University of Toronto Fitness Trainer. I prefer a science-based approach to focus on these & other areas in my life to stay humble & hungry to evolve. I hope you enjoy my work and I'd love to hear your feedback.

- It's a great day to be alive!
Sensei Paul David

Scan & Follow/Like/Subscribe: Facebook, Instagram, YouTube: @senseipublishing

Scan using your phone/iPad camera for Social Media

Visit us at www.senseipublishing.com and sign up for our newsletter to learn more about our exciting books and to experience our FREE Guided Meditations for Kids & Adults.

www.ingramcontent.com/pod-product-compliance
Lightning Source LLC
Chambersburg PA
CBRC091723070526
44585CB00008B/158